EASY AND HEALTHY
INDIAN COOKING

To Tanya
From.
Anita Mallick

ANITA MALLICK

ISBN 979-8-88616-381-0 (paperback)
ISBN 979-8-88616-382-7 (digital)

Christian Faith Publishing
832 Park Avenue
Meadville, PA 16335
www.christianfaithpublishing.com

Printed in the United States of America

I came to the United States in the year 1985 as the wife of an international student from India. In those days there were hardly any Indian grocery stores or restaurants. Now there are many in number. As a result, people are getting the opportunity of enjoying Indian cuisine and are getting interested in knowing about it. For the last ten years, I have been teaching adult and youth Indian cooking classes in public schools under the umbrella of community education. In my classes, I see a lot of interest in learning about this cuisine. This positive classroom experience has sowed in me the idea of writing a cookbook. And then when the pandemic hit, I thought, *Nothing can be better than writing while stuck at home*. Finally, it is here.

While growing up in an extended family in Calcutta, India, I had the opportunity of spending a significant amount of my day with my grandmother. In India, people express their love for others through feeding. And those people could be anybody—your family members, your friends, your neighbors, and even strangers. My grandmother was no exception. In the 1960s, when I was growing up in India, there was no concept of a precooked meal, frozen dinner, or leftover since there was no refrigerator. I grew up eating four fresh home-cooked meals every day. Every meal had to be prepared right before you ate. Ladies used to be in the kitchen almost all day. My grandmother's love of cooking and feeding people used to amaze me. She taught me at an early age that food is love. Food turns out to be the best when you add lots of love to it. I loved everything she cooked. I loved watching her cook. At the age of ten, that was my introduction to cooking. That was how I developed my love for cooking.

It's been forty years since I started cooking for my family and friends. My recipes include mostly what I grew up eating. But after living in the States for the last thirty-five years, my recipes got a global touch and hence did not remain 100 percent authentic. For the most part, Indian cuisine is prepared on the stove top and not in the oven. For that reason, while cooking it is not necessary to strictly measure the ingredients the way we do while baking. My grandmother used to give a little bit of this and a little bit of that, and every time the dish turned out to be the same. Till today I follow my grandmother's method only. I am not a very big follower of a recipe book. Every time I go to a restaurant or people's houses for lunch or dinner, I come home and try to make the dish based on the taste and the look of the dish I remember. I keep trying until I am happy with the end result. Some of my recipes are totally the outcome of my experiments. I believe the most important requirement behind your success as a cook is not to be intimidated. Cooking is an artistic creation, and there is no such thing as right or wrong in art. If it does not turn out to be what you expected it to be, you can always modify the dish. I do it all the time. Like any other skill, the more you cook, the better you will get. So be brave and jump right in.

My recipes are very easy to follow. Ingredients are less expensive. I hope my book will motivate both adults and the younger generation to incorporate home-cooked meals into their daily lives. I am used to cooking with fresh vegetables and herbs. You can use frozen or canned ones, too, if you may choose to do so. Ingredients that you will need to cook Indian dishes are vegetable oil, turmeric powder, cumin powder, coriander powder, fresh or powdered chili, garam masala powder, cinnamon sticks, small cardamom pods, cloves, fresh or powdered ginger, fresh or powdered garlic, and fresh coriander leaves. Most of these ingredients are available in any supermarket and in all Indian grocery stores. In India lunch or dinner includes either homemade bread or rice, dal or lentil soup, a vegetable dish, either meat or fish, and some chutney or yogurt. In Calcutta people eat curries with a store-bought loaf of bread also. An evening snack with tea is something to look forward to. In Calcutta, people eat sweets or desserts not only after dinner but at any time of the day. No wonder Calcutta is known as the diabetes capital of the world.

Now there are a few tips I would like to share with you:

All these recipes can be cooked in saucepans, woks, and frying pans. Always use medium or low heat while cooking. If the heat is high, the spices will burn at the bottom, and the dish will not be edible anymore. The very important part of Indian cooking is stirring. The more you stir, the better all ingredients get fried and mixed together, and you get the authentic taste and aroma you are looking for. Always try to put a lid on while cooking so that the oil and spices stay inside the pot and not in the air. That way cooking time will also be less. Before starting to cook, always prepare everything—such as cutting vegetables or meat, preparing spices, etc.—ahead of time. While cooking, you will not have much time to switch from one ingredient to the other. Always keep a cup of water next to you. While stirring the ingredients, if you see it is getting stuck at the bottom, add two to four tablespoons of water as needed.

None of my recipes require cream or cheese. As a result, the dishes are low in calories.

Dal or Lentil Soup

1 cup red or masoor dal
1 small onion, thinly sliced
4 tablespoons oil
1 teaspoon salt or to taste
1/2 teaspoon turmeric powder
1 whole dry red chili or 1 teaspoon chili flakes

Wash and rinse the dal in a pan. Add 4 cups of hot water, salt, and turmeric. Boil for 15 minutes in medium heat without the lid. Heat up oil in a frying pan. Break the chili into two pieces. Fry them for a minute and add the onion. Fry until golden brown. Pour everything into the dal, and mix well. Cook for 5 more minutes in medium heat. Let it stand. Serve with hot rice and lime wedges.

Spicy Red Dal

1 cup red dal
1 small onion, thinly sliced
2 garlic cloves, grated or chopped
2 medium tomatoes, chopped
2 tablespoons sambar masala
1/2 teaspoon chili powder
1/2 teaspoon turmeric powder
1 teaspoon salt or to taste

1/2 teaspoon sugar
4 tablespoons oil
1 tablespoon ghee or butter
1/2 cup thinly chopped cilantro or coriander leaves

Wash and rinse the dal in a pan and add 4 cups of hot water, salt, and turmeric. Mix well. Boil in medium heat for 15 minutes without cover. Heat up oil in a frying pan and fry the onion until golden brown. Add the garlic and fry for a minute. Add the other ingredients, except butter and cilantro. Mix very well for 2 minutes. Pour everything into the pan, and mix well. Boil for 5 more minutes. Add butter and cilantro. Mix and serve with hot rice and lime wedges.

Plain Red Dal

1 cup red dal
1 medium onion, sliced
2 fresh green chilies
1/2 teaspoon salt or to taste
2 tablespoons butter or ghee

Wash and rinse the dal in a pan. Add 3 cups of hot water and salt. Boil for 15 minutes in medium heat uncovered. Add the sliced onion and chilies. Mix well. Cook for another 5 minutes on medium heat. Add butter and mix. Enjoy.

Mung or Yellow Dal with Peas

1 cup dal
1 cup peas
2 tablespoons oil
1/4 teaspoon cumin seeds
2 tablespoons ginger paste or powder
1 teaspoon salt or to taste
1/2 teaspoon turmeric powder
1/2 teaspoon sugar
1 dry red chili or 1 teaspoon chili flakes
1 tablespoon butter or ghee
Dry spices: 1 bay leaf, 1 medium cinnamon stick, 2 cloves, 2 cardamom pods

Heat up the pan and dry-roast the yellow dal until it turns light brown. Let it cool. Wash and rinse the dal. Set aside. Break the red chili into two pieces. Heat up oil in a pan. Add cumin seeds, chilies, and all the other dry spices and fry for 2 minutes. Add the dal, the rest of the ingredients except peas, and 4 cups of hot water. Boil for 15 minutes in medium heat without the lid. Add peas, and mix well. Cook for another 5 minutes on medium heat. Add butter, and mix well. Let it stand and enjoy.

You can replace peas with zucchini, cabbage, beet, or carrot. If you decide to use these vegetables, cut them into 1-inch-size pieces. Follow the same instructions except at the end, cook for 10 minutes instead of 5.

Mung or Yellow Dal with Tomatoes (Serves Four)

1 cup dal
2 medium tomatoes, chopped
2 tablespoons oil
1 teaspoon salt or to taste

1/4 teaspoon sugar
1/2 teaspoon turmeric powder
1 dry red chili or 1 teaspoon chili flakes
1/4 teaspoon mustard seeds

   Heat up the pan and dry-roast the dal. Let it cool. Wash and rinse the dal. Set aside. Heat up oil in a pan. Break the chili into two pieces. Add chilies and mustard seeds to the pan and fry for a minute. Add the dal, 4 cups of hot water, and the other ingredients. Boil for 15 minutes in medium heat without the lid. Mix well and let it rest. Serve with hot rice.

Spicy Yellow Dal

1 cup mung dal
1 medium onion, thinly sliced
1 medium tomato, chopped

1 tablespoon ginger paste or powder
1 tablespoon garlic paste or powder
1 teaspoon cumin powder
1 teaspoon coriander powder
1/2 teaspoon turmeric powder
1 tablespoon garam masala
4 tablespoons oil
2 green chilies, slit in the middle
1 teaspoon salt or to taste
1/2 teaspoon sugar
1 tablespoon butter or ghee

Heat up the pan and dry-roast the dal. Let it cool and wash and rinse. Add 4 cups of hot water, salt, and turmeric and boil for 15 minutes in medium heat without the lid. Heat up oil in a pan. Fry the onion until golden brown. Add ginger and garlic pastes and fry for a minute. Add all the other ingredients except butter. Mix everything in medium heat until it looks dry and oil shows up. Sprinkle little water if the mixture starts to get stuck at the bottom. Pour it into the boiled dal, and mix well. Cook for 5 more minutes. Add butter and serve.

Chana Dal

1 cup chana dal
2 tablespoons ginger paste or powder
1/2 teaspoon turmeric powder
1/2 teaspoon roasted cumin powder
2 tablespoons chopped fresh coconut or coconut flakes
2 tablespoons raisins
1 teaspoon salt or to taste
1 teaspoon sugar or to taste

4 tablespoons oil
1 tablespoon ghee or butter
Dry spices: 1/4 teaspoon cumin seeds, 1 bay leaf, 1 whole dry red chili broken into two pieces, 1 1-inch-size cinnamon stick, 2 cloves, 2 cardamom pods

Wash and rinse the dal. Add 3 cups of hot water, salt, and turmeric. Mix well and pressure-cook for 10 minutes. Set aside. Heat up oil in a pan and fry all the dry spices for 2 minutes. Add the coconut and raisins and fry for a minute. Add the ginger paste and all other ingredients except cumin and butter and mix for a minute. Pour the spice mix into the cooker, and mix well. Cook in medium heat for 5 more minutes. Add cumin and butter, and mix well. Let it rest. Enjoy with paratha or luchi.

Sambar (Dal in South Indian Style)

1 cup red dal
1 medium onion, cubed
1 1/2 cups mixed vegetables (fresh or frozen)

1/4 cup curry leaves (available in Indian grocery stores)
2 tablespoons oil
6 tablespoons sambar masala (available in Indian stores)
1 teaspoon tamarind paste (available in Indian stores)
1 tablespoon salt or to taste
1/2 teaspoon turmeric
1/2 teaspoon sugar
1 tablespoon ghee or butter

Wash the dal in a pan and add 4 cups of water and salt and turmeric. Mix well. Boil for 10 minutes in medium heat without the lid. Add all vegetables, and mix well. Boil for 10 more minutes in medium heat. Set aside. Heat up oil in a frying pan. Fry the curry leaves for 2 seconds, and add in the dal. Add all other ingredients except ghee, and mix well. Boil for another 5 minutes. Add ghee, and mix well. Serve hot with plain rice.

Garbanzo Beans Curry

2 cups beans
1 1/2 medium onions, sliced
1 medium tomato, chopped
6 tablespoons oil
2 tablespoons ginger paste or powder
2 tablespoons garlic paste or powder
1 teaspoon cumin powder
1 teaspoon coriander powder
3/4 teaspoon turmeric powder
1/2 teaspoon chili powder
1 teaspoon garam masala
1 1/2 teaspoon of salt or to taste

1/2 teaspoon sugar
1 tablespoon ketchup
1/2 cup thinly chopped cilantro

    Soak beans in hot water for an hour. Wash and rinse. Add 4 cups of water, salt, and turmeric and pressure-cook for 20 minutes. Set aside. Heat up oil in a frying pan and fry onions until golden brown. Add ginger and garlic pastes and stir for a minute. Add all the other ingredients except ketchup and cilantro. Mix well in medium heat until it looks dry and oil comes out. Sprinkle little water if the spices start getting stuck at the bottom. Check the amount of water in the beans. Throw away extra water from the pan, leaving only 1 cup. Add all the cooked spices and ketchup to the beans, and mix well. Pressure-cook for another 5 minutes. Sprinkle cilantro. Let it sit. Enjoy with naan, paratha, or puffed bread.

    The same recipe can also be used for black and kidney beans.

VEGETABLES

Potato Curry (Aloo Dum)

4 medium potatoes
1 medium onion, thinly sliced
1 medium tomato, chopped
1 tablespoon garlic paste or garlic powder
1 tablespoon ginger paste or ginger powder
6 tablespoons oil
1 teaspoon salt or to taste
1 teaspoon cumin powder

1 teaspoon coriander powder
1 teaspoon garam masala
1/2 teaspoon turmeric powder
1/2 teaspoon chili powder
1 tablespoon ketchup
4 tablespoons chopped cilantro

Cut each potato into four pieces. Boil them for 10 minutes in high heat without the lid. Cool off and peel them. Set aside. Heat up oil in a pan and fry the onion until golden brown. Add garlic and ginger pastes and stir for a minute. Add all the other ingredients, except ketchup and cilantro. Mix everything well in medium heat until the spices look dry and oil comes out. Sprinkle little water if the spices start getting stuck at the bottom. Add the boiled potatoes and ketchup. Stir well for 2 minutes. Pour 1 cup of water, and mix well. Boil for 5 minutes in low heat with the lid on. Sprinkle cilantro. Let it rest. Enjoy.

The same dish can be prepared using small whole potatoes, fresh or canned. It can also be made without onion and garlic.

Fried Potatoes and Green Onions (Serves Four)

2 medium potatoes
8 sticks of green onion
6 tablespoons oil
1/2 teaspoon salt or to taste
1/2 teaspoon turmeric powder
1/2 teaspoon chili flakes
1/4 teaspoon kalanji or black zeera (optional)

Slice each potato vertically into six pieces. Cut each slice horizontally into ten pieces. Chop green onion sticks into 1-inch-size pieces. Heat up oil in a pan. Add the zeera and fry for a minute. Add everything except green onions and chili. Cook in low heat for 10 minutes with the lid on, stirring occasionally. Add green onions and chili. Mix everything well for 5 more minutes without the lid. Let it rest and enjoy with roti and paratha.

Baked Cauliflower (Serves Four)

1 cauliflower, broken into 2-inch-size florets
1 1/2 medium onions, sliced
1 medium tomato, chopped
1 tablespoon ginger paste or powder
1 tablespoon garlic paste or powder
1 teaspoon cumin powder
1 teaspoon coriander powder
1/2 teaspoon chili powder
1 teaspoon garam masala
8 tablespoons oil
1 teaspoon salt or to taste
1 teaspoon turmeric powder
1 tablespoon ketchup
1/2 cup chopped cilantro

Marinate the cauliflower pieces with 1/2 teaspoon of salt and 1/2 teaspoon of turmeric for 10 minutes. Pat dry the cauliflower pieces with a paper towel. Heat up 4 tablespoons of oil in a pan. Fry the cauliflower pieces for 5 minutes in medium heat, and set them aside. Add the rest of the oil and fry the sliced onions until golden brown. Add garlic and ginger pastes. Stir for a minute. Add all the other ingredients, except cilantro. Mix everything well in medium heat until the mixture looks dry and oil comes out. Sprinkle little water if the spices start getting stuck at the bottom. Add the cauliflower pieces, and mix well. Add 1 cup of water, and mix well. Transfer everything to a baking pan. Bake uncovered for 10 minutes at 350 degrees. Sprinkle cilantro and serve.

Cauliflower and Potato Curry (Serves Six)

1 cauliflower, cut into 1-inch-size pieces
2 medium potatoes, peeled and cubed into 1/2-inch-size pieces
1/2 cup peas
1 medium onion, sliced
1 medium tomato, chopped
1 tablespoon ginger paste or powder
1 tablespoon garlic paste or powder
1 teaspoon cumin powder
1 teaspoon coriander powder
1 teaspoon turmeric powder
1/2 teaspoon chili powder
1 teaspoon garam masala

1 teaspoon salt or to taste
1/2 teaspoon sugar
6 tablespoons oil
1 tablespoon ketchup
1/2 cup chopped cilantro

Heat up oil in a pan and add the cauliflower, potatoes, and onion. Fry them, adding salt and turmeric, until golden brown. Add ginger and garlic pastes and stir for a minute. Add all the other ingredients, except chopped cilantro. Mix everything well in medium heat until the mixture is dry and oil comes out. Sprinkle little water if the mixture starts getting stuck at the bottom. Pour 1 cup of water, and mix well. Cook for 10 minutes in low heat with the lid on. Add cilantro. Let it stand and enjoy.

Potato and Cauliflower Fry (Serves Six)

1 medium cauliflower
2 medium potatoes
1/2 teaspoon salt or to taste
1/2 teaspoon turmeric powder
1/4 cup oil
1 whole dry red chili broken into two pieces or 1/2 teaspoon crushed chili

Cut the cauliflower into 1-inch-size pieces. Peel and dice potatoes into 1/2-inch-size pieces. Heat up oil in a pan and fry chilies for a minute. Add the vegetables, salt, and turmeric. Cook in medium heat for 10 minutes, stirring occasionally. Add 4 tablespoons of water, and mix well. Cook for 5 minutes in low heat with the lid on. Let it rest. Serve.

Fried Cut Beans (Serves Four)

1 pound frozen or fresh cut beans
1/2 teaspoon salt or to taste
1/2 teaspoon turmeric powder
1 teaspoon garlic paste or powder
1 teaspoon crushed chili
4 tablespoons oil

Cut the fresh beans into 1-inch-size pieces. If frozen beans are being used, there's no need to thaw them. Heat up oil in a pan. Add all the other ingredients and mix everything well for a minute. Add the beans. Fry everything well for 5 minutes. Add 1/2 cup of water. Mix well. Cook in medium heat with the lid on for 10 minutes. Set aside and enjoy.

Beans and Potato Curry (Serves Four)

1/2 pound fresh or frozen cut beans
2 medium potatoes, diced small
2 medium tomatoes, chopped
6 tablespoons oil
1 teaspoon salt or to taste
1/4 teaspoon sugar
1 tablespoon ginger paste or powder
1 teaspoon cumin powder
1 teaspoon coriander powder
1/2 teaspoon turmeric powder
1/2 teaspoon chili powder
1/2 teaspoon garam masala
1 tablespoon ketchup

Cut the fresh beans into 1-inch-size pieces. If frozen beans are being used, there's no need to thaw them. Heat up oil in a pan and fry the vegetables for 5 minutes, adding salt and turmeric. Add all the other ingredients except ketchup and mix everything well for 5 minutes in medium heat. Add ketchup and 1 cup of water, and mix well. Cook in low heat for 10 minutes with the lid on. Let it stand and serve with hot rice.

Okra Masala (Serves Four)

1 pound fresh or frozen cut or whole okra
1 medium onion, chopped.
1 tablespoon ginger paste or powder
1 tablespoon garlic paste or powder
1 medium tomato, chopped

6 tablespoons oil
1/2 teaspoon turmeric powder
1/2 teaspoon cumin powder
1/2 teaspoon coriander powder
1/2 teaspoon garam masala
1/2 teaspoon chili powder
3/4 teaspoon salt or to taste
1 teaspoon ketchup

Cut fresh okra into 1/2-inch-size pieces. If frozen okra is being used, there's no need to thaw them. Heat up 4 table-spoons of oil in a frying pan and add okra, salt, and turmeric. Keep frying until dry. Set it aside. Heat up the rest of the oil and fry the chopped onion until golden brown. Add ginger and garlic pastes. Stir for a minute. Add all the other ingredients and keep stirring in medium heat until the mixture is dry and oil comes out. Sprinkle little water if the mixture starts getting stuck at the bottom. Add okra and 1/2 cup of water, and mix well. Cook for 5 minutes in medium heat, stirring occasionally. Let it rest. Enjoy.

Fried Okra (Serves Four)

1 pound fresh or frozen cut okra
6 tablespoons vegetable oil
1/2 teaspoon salt or to taste
1/2 teaspoon turmeric

Cut fresh okra into 1/2-inch-size pieces. If frozen okra is being used, there's no need to thaw them. Heat up oil in a frying pan. Add the okra, salt, and turmeric powder and cook for 10 minutes on medium heat, mixing occasionally. Turn the heat to low and cook for another 5 minutes, stirring frequently. Let it stand and serve.

Fried Eggplant (Serves Four)

1 medium eggplant
1/2 teaspoon salt or to taste
1/2 teaspoon turmeric powder
1/2 cup oil

Slice the eggplant vertically in the middle. Again slice each portion into three pieces vertically. Rub them with salt and turmeric. Set aside for 10 minutes. Pat dry the pieces using a paper towel. Heat up half of the oil in a frying pan and place the eggplant slices on the pan. Fry them for 3 minutes in medium heat with the lid on. Turn sides and add the rest of the oil. Fry them the same way. Take them out, and enjoy them with hot rice or chapati.

Eggplant with Yogurt

1 medium eggplant
3/4 teaspoon turmeric powder
1 tablespoon cumin powder
1 tablespoon coriander powder
1/2 teaspoon chili powder
1 tablespoon ginger paste or powder
3/4 cup yogurt
1 1/2 teaspoons salt or to taste
1 teaspoon sugar
1/2 cup oil
1 tablespoon ketchup

Slice the eggplant in the middle horizontally. Take one portion and cut it into four slices vertically. Take one slice at a time and cut it into four more slices vertically and repeat. Marinate them with 1/2 teaspoon of salt and 1/2 teaspoon of turmeric powder. Set aside for 10 minutes. Pat dry with a paper towel. Mix yogurt very well and set aside. Heat up 4 tablespoons of oil in a frying pan. Spread it all over the pan. Place half of the eggplant pieces in the pan and fry them in medium heat on each side for 2 minutes. Take them out. Again add 4 more tablespoons of oil to the pan, and fry the rest of the eggplant pieces the same way. Take them out. Pour the rest of the oil and add all the ingredients except yogurt and ketchup. Mix the ingredients in medium heat until the mixture is dry and oil comes out. Add yogurt and ketchup and mix everything well. Add 1 cup of water, and mix well. Place the fried eggplants in the gravy. Cook for 10 minutes in low heat without the lid. Let it stand. Enjoy with rice or bread.

Potatoes, Eggplant, and Shrimp

1/2 pound medium shrimp, cleaned
2 medium potatoes, diced into 1/2-inch-size pieces
1/2 eggplant, diced into 1-inch-size pieces
1 medium onion, diced
4 tablespoons mustard or any type of oil
3/4 teaspoon salt or to taste
1/2 teaspoon turmeric powder
2 whole dry chilies, broken in the middle

Mix everything in a pan, adding 1/4 cup of water. Cook in low heat for 15 minutes with the lid on. Stir every 5 minutes, making sure that it is not getting stuck at the bottom. Sprinkle some more water if needed. Mix well. Let it rest. Serve with hot rice.

Sautéed Spinach and Peas

1 bunch fresh spinach, chopped
1/2 cup peas
1 teaspoon garlic paste or powder
1/2 teaspoon crushed chili
4 tablespoons oil
1/2 teaspoon salt or to taste
1/2 teaspoon turmeric

Wash and rinse the spinach thoroughly. Pat dry with a paper towel. Chop and set aside. Heat up oil in a pan. Add the chili and fry for 2 seconds. Add the garlic and fry for another 2 seconds. Add the vegetables and other ingredients and cook for 10 minutes on medium heat, stirring occasionally. Serve with hot rice. You can also use garbanzo beans instead of peas.

The same recipe can be used for kale, mustard, or collard greens also. These leaves take a little longer to cook. Cook them in medium heat with the lid on for 15 minutes, stirring occasionally.

Asparagus and Shrimp Masala (Serves Four)

1 pound asparagus, broken into 1-inch-size pieces
1/2 pound medium shrimp, cleaned
1 medium onion, thinly sliced
1 tablespoon ginger paste or powder
1 tablespoon garlic paste or powder
6 tablespoons oil
3/4 teaspoon turmeric
1 teaspoon cumin powder
1 teaspoon coriander powder
1/2 teaspoon chili powder

1 teaspoon salt or to taste
1 tablespoon ketchup

Peel and clean the shrimp. Heat up oil in a pan and fry the sliced onion until golden brown. Add asparagus pieces, salt, and turmeric. Fry for 5 minutes in medium heat. Add ginger and garlic pastes and stir for a minute. Add all the other ingredients except ketchup. Mix everything well in medium heat until oil comes out. Sprinkle little water if the mixture starts getting stuck at the bottom. Add the shrimp, 1/2 cup of water, and ketchup. Mix everything well. Cook for another 10 minutes in low heat with the lid on. Let it rest. Enjoy.

Sautéed Zucchini (Serves Four)

4 medium zucchini
1 tablespoon ginger paste or powder
1 green chili, thinly sliced
1/2 teaspoon turmeric
1/2 teaspoon salt or to taste
1/4 teaspoon sugar
4 tablespoons oil

Grate zucchini and squeeze the water out. Heat up oil in a frying pan. Add zucchini and all the other ingredients. Cook in medium heat for 10 minutes with the lid on, stirring occasionally. Take the lid off, and mix well, stirring for another 5 minutes. Enjoy.

The same recipe can be used for daikon.

Sautéed Broccoli Florets

1 broccoli, separated into 2-inch-size florets
2 tablespoons oil
1/2 teaspoon garlic paste or powder
1/2 teaspoon chili flakes
1/4 teaspoon salt

    Heat up oil in a frying pan. Add the garlic and chili flakes and quick-fry for a second or 2. Add the broccoli and salt, and mix well. Cook for 5 minutes in low heat with the lid on. Take the lid off, and mix well. Let it rest. Serve hot.

Zucchini and Shrimp Curry (Serves Four)

4 medium zucchini, diced into 1-inch-size pieces
2 medium potatoes, diced into 1/2-inch-size pieces
1/2 pound medium shrimp
4 tablespoons oil
1 tablespoon ginger paste or powder
1 teaspoon cumin powder
1 teaspoon coriander powder
1/2 teaspoon turmeric powder
1/2 teaspoon garam masala
1/2 teaspoon chili powder
1 teaspoon salt
1/4 teaspoon sugar
1 tablespoon ketchup

Peel and wash shrimps thoroughly, and set them aside. Heat up oil in a pan and add the vegetables, 1/2 teaspoon of salt, and 1/4 teaspoon of turmeric. Fry for 5 minutes in medium heat. Add all the other ingredients except ketchup and mix everything well in medium heat until oil comes out. Sprinkle little water if the mixture starts getting stuck at the bottom. Add the shrimp and ketchup. Mix everything well. Add 1 cup of water, and mix well. Cook for 10 minutes in low heat with the lid on. Set aside. Serve with hot rice.

Squash with Garbanzo Beans (Serves Four)

1 medium-size butternut or acorn squash (serves four)
2 medium potatoes
1/2 can garbanzo beans
6 tablespoons oil
1 tablespoon ginger paste or powder
1 teaspoon cumin powder
1 teaspoon coriander powder
1 teaspoon garam masala
1 teaspoon chili powder
3/4 teaspoon turmeric powder
1 teaspoon salt or to taste
1/2 teaspoon sugar

Peel and cut the squash into 1-inch-size cubes. Peel and cut the potatoes into 1/2-inch-size cubes. Wash the canned beans to get rid of the salt. Set them aside. Heat up oil in a pan and fry the vegetables for 5 minutes in medium heat, adding 1/2 teaspoon of salt and 1/2 teaspoon of turmeric. Add all the other ingredients and mix everything well for 5 minutes in medium heat. Add 1 cup of water, and mix well. Cook for 10 minutes in low heat with the lid on. Let it rest. Enjoy.

Sautéed Cabbage and Carrot (Serves Four)

1/2 small cabbage, thinly sliced
1 medium carrot, peeled and grated
1 teaspoon ginger paste or powder
1 teaspoon garlic paste or powder
1 fresh chili, thinly sliced, or 1/2 teaspoon chili flakes
4 tablespoons oil

1/2 teaspoon salt or to taste
1/2 cup chopped cilantro

Heat up oil in a frying pan. Add garlic, ginger, and chili and fry for a minute. Add the vegetables, salt, and 1/4 cup of water, and mix well. Cook for 5 minutes in low heat with the lid on. Take the lid off and cook for another 5 minutes in medium heat, stirring frequently. Add cilantro, and mix well. Set aside and serve.

Cabbage and Shrimp Curry (Serves Four)

1 small cabbage, thinly sliced
2 medium potatoes, diced small
1/2 pound medium shrimp, peeled and washed
1 medium onion, sliced thin
1 medium tomato, chopped
6 tablespoons oil
1 1/2 tablespoons ginger paste or powder
1 teaspoon turmeric powder
1 teaspoon cumin powder
1 teaspoon coriander powder
1 teaspoon chili powder
1 teaspoon garam masala
1 teaspoon salt
1/2 teaspoon sugar

Heat up oil in a pan. Add potatoes and onion slices and fry for 5 minutes in medium heat. Add all the other ingredients, and mix well for 2 minutes. Add the chopped cabbage, and mix well. Sprinkle 1/2 cup of water all over the cabbage. Mix well. Cook in low heat for 10 minutes with the lid on. Add the shrimp and mix everything well. Cook for 10 more minutes in medium heat without the lid, stirring frequently. Let it stand and enjoy.

Potato and Peas Curry (Serves Four)

2 medium potatoes, peeled and diced
1 cup peas
1 medium tomato, chopped
4 tablespoons oil
1 tablespoon ginger paste or powder
1 teaspoon cumin powder
1 teaspoon coriander powder
1/2 teaspoon chili powder
1/2 teaspoon turmeric powder
3/4 teaspoon salt or to taste
1/2 teaspoon sugar
1 tablespoon ketchup

Heat up oil in a pan and add the potatoes, peas, 1/2 teaspoon of salt, and 1/4 teaspoon of turmeric. Fry for 5 minutes in medium heat. Add all the other ingredients and mix everything well for 5 minutes. Add 1 cup of water, and mix well. Cook for 10 minutes in low heat with the lid on. Let it rest and enjoy.

Raw Jackfruit and Potato Curry (Serves Four)

1 can jackfruit (available in oriental grocery stores)
2 medium potatoes, peeled and diced
2 medium onions, sliced
1 medium tomato, chopped
1 1/2 tablespoons ginger paste or powder
1 1/2 tablespoons garlic paste or powder
6 tablespoons oil

1 tablespoon cumin powder
1 tablespoon coriander powder
1 teaspoon turmeric powder
1 teaspoon chili powder
1 teaspoon garam masala
1 teaspoon salt or to taste
1 tablespoon ketchup
1/2 cup thinly chopped cilantro
1 tablespoon butter or ghee

Wash the canned jackfruit thoroughly to get rid of the salt and dry them. Cut the pieces into 1 inch. Set them aside. Heat up oil in a pan. Fry the sliced onions until golden brown. Add the jackfruit, potatoes, 1/2 teaspoon of salt, and 1/2 teaspoon of turmeric powder and fry in medium heat for 5 minutes. Add ginger and garlic pastes and stir for a minute. Add all the other ingredients except ketchup, cilantro, and butter. Mix everything well until it looks dry and oil comes out. Sprinkle little water if it starts getting stuck at the bottom. Add 1 1/2 cups of water and ketchup, and mix well. Cook in low heat for 15 minutes with the lid on. Add butter and cilantro. Let it stand. Enjoy.

This dish looks like goat or mutton curry. Hence, it is also called tree goat curry in Calcutta. It is a very popular dish among both vegetarians and nonvegetarians in Calcutta.

Green Papaya in Mustard Sauce (Serves Four)

1 medium green papaya
4 tablespoons white mustard seeds
4 tablespoons oil
3/4 teaspoon salt or to taste
3/4 teaspoon turmeric
1/2 teaspoon chili powder
1/2 teaspoon sugar
1 tablespoon ketchup

Soak mustard seeds in 6 tablespoons of water for 1/2 hour. Blend it to a paste. Peel and clean the inside of the papaya. Dice it into 1/2-inch-size pieces. Heat up oil in a pan. Add the papaya, salt, and turmeric and fry them in medium heat for 5 minutes. Add all the other ingredients except the mustard paste, and mix well. Add the mustard paste and 1 1/2 cups of water, and mix well. Cook for 20 minutes in low heat with the lid on. Set aside and enjoy with hot rice.

MEAT AND POULTRY

Chicken Curry with Potatoes (Serves Four)

2 pounds chicken with or without bones
2 medium potatoes, peeled and cut in half
2 medium onions, sliced
1 medium tomato, chopped
6 tablespoons oil
1 1/2 teaspoons salt or to taste
1 tablespoon ginger paste or powder
1 tablespoon garlic paste or powder
1 teaspoon cumin powder
1 teaspoon coriander powder
1 teaspoon chili powder
1 teaspoon turmeric powder
1 teaspoon garam masala
1 tablespoon ketchup

Cut chicken into 2-inch-size pieces. Marinate it with 1 teaspoon of salt and 1/2 teaspoon of turmeric. Set aside for an hour. Heat up oil in a pan. Fry onion slices until golden brown. Add ginger and garlic pastes and fry for a minute. Add all the other ingredients except ketchup and potatoes. Fry them on medium heat for 5 minutes. Add the chicken pieces and mix everything well in medium heat with the lid on, stirring occasionally until the chicken looks dry and oil comes out. Sprinkle little water if the mixture gets stuck at the bottom. The more you mix, the better the taste will be. Add ketchup, potatoes, and 1 1/2 cups of water. Mix everything well. Cook in low heat with the lid on for 20 minutes. Set aside. Enjoy.

Yogurt Chicken (Serves Four)

2 pounds chicken with or without bones
2 medium onions, sliced
1 medium tomato, chopped
6 tablespoons oil
1 tablespoon ginger paste or powder
1 tablespoon garlic paste or powder
1 teaspoon cumin powder

1 teaspoon coriander powder
1 teaspoon turmeric
1 teaspoon chili powder
1 teaspoon garam masala
1/2 cup yogurt
1 1/2 teaspoons salt or to taste
1/2 teaspoon sugar
1 tablespoon ketchup

Cut chicken into 2-inch-size pieces and marinate with 1 teaspoon of salt and 1/2 teaspoon of turmeric. Set aside. Beat yogurt so that there will not be any lump. Heat up oil and fry the onion slices until golden brown. Add ginger and garlic pastes and fry for a minute. Add all the other ingredients except yogurt, garam masala, and ketchup. Mix everything well in medium heat for 5 minutes. Add the chicken pieces. Mix everything with the lid on in medium heat, stirring occasionally until the mixture looks dry and oil comes out. The more you mix the ingredients, the better the taste will be. Sprinkle little water if the mixture starts getting stuck at the bottom. Pour the yogurt gradually and stir constantly. Add garam masala and ketchup. Mix everything well. Pour 1 1/2 cups of water, and mix well. Cook for 20 minutes in low heat with the lid on. Let it rest and serve with hot rice.

Baked Chicken (Serves Four)

8 drumsticks
1 medium onion, sliced
6 tablespoons oil
1 tablespoon ginger paste or powder
1 tablespoon garlic paste or powder
3/4 teaspoon turmeric
1 teaspoon cumin powder
1 teaspoon coriander powder

1/2 teaspoon chili powder
1 teaspoon garam masala
1 teaspoon salt or to taste
1 tablespoon ketchup
2 tablespoons chopped cilantro

Make small cuts on each leg so that spices can go in. Rub them with 1/2 teaspoon of salt and 1/2 teaspoon of turmeric. Set aside for 10 minutes. Heat up 2 tablespoons of oil in a frying pan and spread oil all over the pan. Place the drumsticks in the pan and fry them in medium heat for 2 minutes on each side. Set them aside. Heat up the rest of the oil and fry the onion until golden brown. Add ginger and garlic pastes and fry for a minute. Add all the other ingredients except cilantro. Mix everything well for 5 minutes in medium heat. Add the chicken pieces and 1/2 cup of water. Mix well. Transfer everything to a baking pan and cook uncovered at 350 degrees for 20 minutes. Add cilantro. Let it rest. Enjoy

Tandoori Chicken

1 whole chicken cut into twelve pieces
2 tablespoons ginger paste or powder
2 tablespoons garlic paste or powder
1 teaspoon turmeric powder
1 tablespoon cumin powder
1 tablespoon coriander powder
1 teaspoon chili powder
1 tablespoon garam masala
4 tablespoons oil
1 cup yogurt
4 tablespoons lime juice
1 1/2 tablespoons salt

Remove skin from the chicken and cut it into twelve pieces. Set aside. Mix all ingredients together. Rub the chicken pieces with that spice mix. Keep it covered inside the fridge for 24 hours. Take it out and keep it at room temperature for 2 hours before cooking. Heat up the oven to 400 degrees. Cover the baking pan with foil. Spray oil on the foil. Place the chicken pieces on the tray. Bake for 20 minutes. Throw away the water that has accumulated in the pan. Turn the sides of the chicken pieces. Baste them with the leftover marinade. Bake for another 20 minutes. Take it out and let it rest. Enjoy.

If you want to make it colorful, you may add food color to the spice mix. You can also use store-bought tandoori masala.

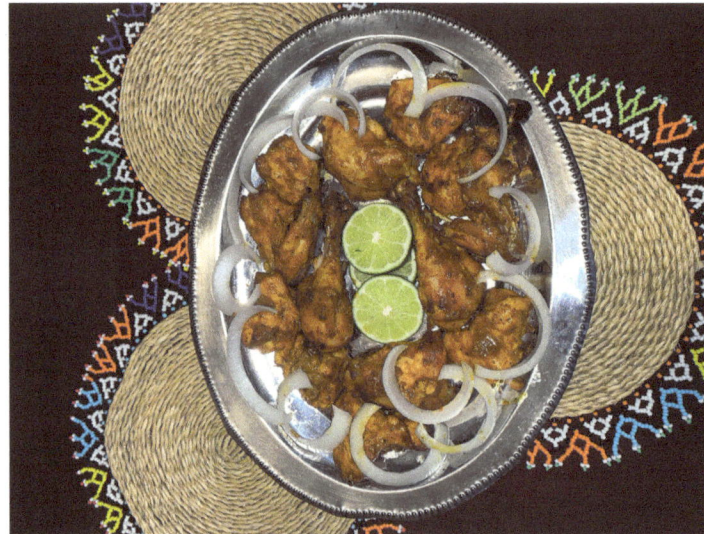

Chicken Roast (Serves Four)

1 whole chicken
4 tablespoons oil
2 tablespoons ginger paste or powder
2 tablespoons garlic paste or powder

1 tablespoon cumin powder
1 tablespoon coriander powder
1 teaspoon chili powder
1 teaspoon turmeric
1 tablespoon garam masala
1 1/2 teaspoons salt
Juice of 1 lime

Wash the chicken well. Take out the skin from the chicken. Pat dry with a paper towel. Poke all over with a knife. Mix all the ingredients and rub the chicken thoroughly with the spice mix. Keep in the fridge overnight. The next day, take it out 2 hours before cooking. Heat up the oven to 400 degrees. Place the chicken in a baking pan. Cover it with foil and bake for 45 minutes. Take the cover out and bake for another 45 minutes, basting the chicken occasionally with the marinade that has accumulated in the pan. Let it rest and serve hot.

Lamb Vindaloo (Serves Four)

2 pounds boneless lamb, cubed
2 medium potatoes, peeled and cubed
2 medium onions, sliced
1 medium tomato, chopped
1/4 cup oil
2 tablespoons ginger paste or powder
2 tablespoons garlic paste or powder
1 tablespoon cumin powder
1 tablespoon coriander powder
1 teaspoon turmeric
1 teaspoon chili powder
1 tablespoon garam masala

1/2 cup yogurt
1 1/2 teaspoons salt or to taste
2 tablespoons ketchup
1/2 cup cilantro

Mix yogurt, 1 tablespoon of ginger, 1 tablespoon of garlic, 1/2 tablespoon of cumin, 1/2 tablespoon of coriander, 1/2 teaspoon of turmeric, 1/2 teaspoon of chili powder, 1/2 tablespoon of garam masala, and 1 teaspoon of salt. Rub lamb pieces thoroughly with the spice mix, and keep them in the fridge overnight. Take it out 2 hours before cooking. Heat up 2 tablespoons of oil in a pan and fry the cubed potatoes in medium heat for 3 minutes. Set them aside. Add the rest of the oil and fry the onions until brown. Add all the other ingredients except cilantro. Mix everything on medium heat with the lid on for 5 minutes. Add the marinated meat and mix everything in medium heat, stirring occasionally until it looks dry and oil comes out. Sprinkle little water if it starts getting stuck at the bottom. The more you stir, the better the taste will be. Add 2 cups of water, and mix well. Cook in low heat for an hour with the lid on. Add fried potatoes, and mix well. Cook for another 10 minutes in low heat with the lid on. Add cilantro. Mix well. Set aside. Enjoy.

Coriander Lamb (Serves Four)

2 pounds boneless lamb, cubed
2 medium onions, sliced
1 medium tomato, chopped
1/4 cup oil
2 tablespoons ginger paste or powder
2 tablespoons garlic paste or powder
1 tablespoon cumin powder
1 tablespoon coriander powder
1 teaspoon turmeric powder
4 green chilies
1/2 cup yogurt

1 1/2 teaspoons salt
1/2 teaspoon sugar
1 cup chopped cilantro
Dry spices: 1 bay leaf, 1 cinnamon stick, 2 cloves, 2 cardamom pods

Blend chilies and cilantro together. Set aside. Mix yogurt, 1 tablespoon of ginger, 1 tablespoon of garlic, 1/2 tablespoon of cumin, 1/2 tablespoon of coriander, 1 teaspoon of turmeric powder, 1 teaspoon of salt, and the cilantro-chili paste. Add lamb pieces to that spice mix, and mix well. Refrigerate for 24 hours. Take it out 2 hours before cooking. Heat up oil in a pan and fry the dry spices for 2 minutes. Add the onion slices and fry them in medium heat until golden brown. Add the remaining ingredients, and mix well for 5 minutes in medium heat. Add the marinated lamb. Mix everything in medium heat with the lid on, stirring occasionally until oil comes out. Sprinkle little water if the mixture starts getting stuck at the bottom. The more you stir, the better the taste will be. Add 2 cups of water, and mix well. Cook in low heat for an hour with the lid on. Set aside and enjoy

The same recipe can also be used for chicken and goat meat. But for chicken, the cooking time in the end will be 20 minutes.

Goat Masala

2 pounds goat meat, cut into 1 1/2-inch-size pieces
2 medium onions, sliced
1 medium tomato, chopped
2 tablespoons ginger paste or powder
2 tablespoons garlic paste or powder
1 tablespoon cumin powder
1 tablespoon coriander powder
1 teaspoon turmeric powder
1 teaspoon chili powder
2 tablespoons yogurt

1 1/2 teaspoons salt
1/4 cup mustard oil or any type
1 tablespoon ketchup
4 tablespoons chopped cilantro
Dry spices: 1 bay leaf, 1 cinnamon stick, 2 cloves, 2 cardamom pods

Marinate the goat meat with yogurt, 1 tablespoon of ginger paste, 1 tablespoon of garlic paste, 1/2 tablespoon of cumin powder, 1/2 tablespoon of coriander powder, 1 teaspoon of turmeric powder, and 1 teaspoon of salt. Set aside for 4 hours. Heat up oil in a pan and add the dry spices. Fry them for 2 minutes. Add the onion slices and fry in medium heat until golden brown. Add the rest of the ingredients except cilantro, and mix well in medium heat for 5 minutes. Add the marinated goat meat and mix everything for 15 minutes in medium heat with the lid on, stirring occasionally. Sprinkle little water if the mixture starts getting stuck at the bottom. The more you stir, the better the taste will be. Add 2 cups of water, and mix well. Pressure-cook for 40 minutes. Let the steam out on its own. Let it stand. Add chopped cilantro. Enjoy.

Goat Meat in Calcutta Style

2 pounds goat meat, cut into 1 1/2-inch-size pieces
2 medium potatoes, cut in half
2 medium onions, thinly sliced
1 medium tomato, chopped
2 tablespoons ginger paste or powder
2 tablespoons garlic paste or powder
1 tablespoon cumin powder
1 tablespoon coriander powder
1 teaspoon chili powder
1 teaspoon turmeric powder
1 1/2 teaspoons salt or to taste

8 tablespoons mustard oil or any type
Dry spices: 1 bay leaf, 1 cinnamon stick, 2 cloves, 2 cardamom pods

Marinate the meat with 1 tablespoon of ginger, 1 tablespoon of garlic, 1 teaspoon of cumin powder, 1 teaspoon of coriander powder, 1 teaspoon of turmeric powder, 1 teaspoon of salt, and 2 tablespoons of mustard oil. Set aside for 4 hours. Heat up the rest of the oil in a pan and fry the dry spices for 2 minutes. Add onion slices and fry until golden brown. Add the rest of the ingredients except potatoes, and mix in medium heat for 5 minutes. Add the marinated meat, and mix well for 15 minutes in medium heat with the lid on, stirring occasionally. Sprinkle little water if the mixture starts getting stuck at the bottom. The longer you stir, the better the taste will be. Add 2 cups of water, and mix well. Pressure-cook for 40 minutes. Let the pressure out on its own. Add potatoes and pressure-cook for another 5 minutes. Let it rest and serve.

Potato and Meatball Curry (Serves Four)

1 pound ground chicken or turkey
2 medium potatoes, diced into pieces 3/4 of an inch in size
1/2 medium onion, minced
1 medium onion, sliced
6 tablespoons oil
1 1/2 tablespoons ginger paste or powder
1 1/2 tablespoons garlic paste or powder
1 teaspoon cumin powder
1 teaspoon coriander powder
1 teaspoon chili powder
1 teaspoon turmeric powder
1 teaspoon garam masala
1 1/2 teaspoons salt or to taste
1 tablespoon ketchup
1/2 cup finely chopped cilantro

Mix the ground meat with the minced onion, 1/2 tablespoon of ginger paste and 1/2 tablespoon of garlic paste, 1/2 teaspoon of chili powder, 1/2 teaspoon of garam masala, 1/2 teaspoon of turmeric, 3/4 teaspoon of salt, 1/2 cup of regular bread crumb, and cilantro. Make 1-inch-size balls. Bake them at 400 degrees for 10 minutes. Set aside. Heat up 2 tablespoons of oil in a pan and fry the diced potatoes for 2 minutes. Set aside. Add the rest of the oil and fry the sliced onion until golden brown. Add ginger and garlic pastes and fry for a minute. Add the rest of the ingredients. Mix in medium heat until it looks dry and oil comes out. Sprinkle some water if the mixture starts getting stuck at the bottom. Add the potatoes, and mix well. Add 1 cup of water, and mix well. Place the meatballs in the gravy. Cook for 10 minutes in low heat with the lid on. Sprinkle cilantro. Let it rest. Enjoy.

FISH

Fried Salmon (Serves Four)

1 pound fresh or frozen salmon fillet
1 teaspoon turmeric
1/2 teaspoon salt
4 tablespoons oil

Cut the fillet into 4-inch-size pieces. Rub them with turmeric and salt. Set aside for 10 minutes. Heat up oil in a pan. Spread oil all over the pan. Add salmon pieces. Fry them in medium heat with the lid on for 3 minutes on each side. Let it rest and serve hot.

The same recipe can also be used for tilapia, sea bass, and cod.

Roasted Salmon (Serves Four)

1 pound salmon fillet (fresh or frozen)
1 teaspoon garlic powder
1 teaspoon ginger powder
1/2 teaspoon cumin powder
1/2 teaspoon coriander powder
1/2 teaspoon turmeric powder
1/4 teaspoon chili powder
1/2 teaspoon garam masala
1/2 teaspoon mustard paste
2 tablespoons lime juice
4 tablespoons oil
3/4 teaspoon salt

Cut the fillet into 4-inch-size pieces. Mix all the ingredients and 2 tablespoons of oil and make a paste. Rub the fish thoroughly with that mix. Set aside for 10 minutes. Heat up the rest of the oil and spread it around the pan.

Roast the fish for 3 minutes on each side in medium heat with the lid on. Let it stand and serve.
The same recipe can also be used for tilapia, sea bass, cod, etc.

Fish Curry (Serves Four)

1 pound tilapia fillet
1 medium onion, thinly sliced
1 medium tomato, chopped
6 tablespoons oil
1 1/2 teaspoon salt or to taste
1 tablespoon ginger paste or powder
1 tablespoon garlic paste or powder

1 1/2 teaspoons turmeric powder
1 teaspoon cumin powder
1 teaspoon coriander powder
1 teaspoon garam masala
1 teaspoon chili powder
1 tablespoon ketchup
1/2 cup thinly chopped cilantro

Cut the fish into 2-inch-size pieces. Marinate them with 1 teaspoon of salt and 1 teaspoon of turmeric. Set aside for 10 minutes. Heat up 2 tablespoons of oil in a frying pan and spread the oil all over the pan. Add the fish and fry them in medium heat for 2 minutes on each side. Set them aside. Add the rest of the oil to the pan and fry the onion until golden brown. Add ginger and garlic pastes and fry for a minute. Add the rest of the ingredients except cilantro and mix in medium heat until the mixture looks dry and oil comes out. Sprinkle little water if the spices start to get stuck at the bottom. Add 3/4 cup of water. Mix everything well and bring it to a boil. Add the fish and cook for 10 minutes in low heat with the lid on. Add cilantro. Let it rest and serve with hot rice.

Baked Fish (Serves Four)

1 pound fillet of fish (any type)
1 teaspoon garlic powder
1/2 teaspoon black pepper
2 tablespoons oil
3/4 teaspoon salt or to taste
2 tablespoons lime juice

Cut the fillet into 6-inch-size pieces. Mix all ingredients together. Rub the fish with the spice mix. Heat up the oven to 400 degrees. Bake the fish for 10 minutes and let it rest. Enjoy.

Salmon with Coconut

1 pound fillet, cut into 4-inch-size pieces
1 cup grated fresh coconut or coconut powder
2 tablespoons white mustard seeds
1 1/2 teaspoon salt
1 teaspoon turmeric
1/4 teaspoon sugar
4 tablespoons mustard or any type of oil
4 fresh green chilies, slit in the middle

Soak the mustard seeds in 4 tablespoons of water for 1/2 hour. Make a paste, blending the seeds. Add the coconut and blend until smooth. Add all the other ingredients, and mix well. Add the salmon pieces and 1/4 cup of water. Mix well. Bake in the microwave oven for 10 minutes on medium power with the lid on. Let it rest and serve with hot rice.

This recipe is also good for shrimp.

Fish in Garlic Sauce

1 pound fish, cut into 2-inch-size pieces
2 medium tomatoes, chopped
2 tablespoons garlic paste or powder
1 tablespoon ginger paste or powder
1 teaspoon cumin powder
1 teaspoon coriander powder
1 teaspoon garam masala
1 teaspoon chili powder
1 1/2 teaspoon turmeric powder
1 1/2 teaspoon salt or to taste

6 tablespoons oil
1 tablespoon ketchup
1/2 cup thinly chopped cilantro

Marinate the fish with 1 teaspoon of salt and 1 teaspoon of turmeric powder for 10 minutes. Heat up 2 tablespoons of oil in a pan. Spread oil all over the pan. Fry the fish on medium heat for 2 minutes on each side. Take them out. Add the rest of the oil and ginger and garlic pastes. Fry for a minute. Add all the other ingredients except cilantro and mix everything in medium heat until the mixture looks dry and oil comes out. Sprinkle little water if the mixture starts getting stuck at the bottom. Add 1 cup of water, and mix well. Place the fish in the pan. Cook for 10 minutes in low heat with the lid on. Add cilantro and let it rest. Enjoy with hot rice.

Fish in Mustard Sauce

1 pound fish, cut into 2-inch-size pieces
3 tablespoons white mustard seeds
1 1/2 teaspoon salt
1 1/2 teaspoon turmeric powder
6 tablespoons oil
1 teaspoon chili powder

Soak the mustard seeds in 1/2 cup of water for an hour. Make a paste. Set aside. Marinate the fish with 1 teaspoon of salt and 1 teaspoon of turmeric powder for 10 minutes. Heat up 2 tablespoons of oil in a pan and spread it all over the pan. Fry the fish on medium heat for 2 minutes on each side. Take out the fish, and set it aside. Heat up the rest of the oil and add all the other ingredients and 1 cup of water. Mix well. Place the fried fish in the pan and cook in low heat for 10 minutes with the lid on. Let it rest, and enjoy it with hot rice.

Salmon in Yogurt

1 pound salmon fillet or steak, cut into 4-inch-size pieces
1/2 cup yogurt
2 tablespoons white mustard seeds
4 green chilies, slit in the middle
4 tablespoons mustard or any other oil
1 1/2 teaspoon salt
1 1/2 teaspoon turmeric powder
1/4 teaspoon sugar
1 tablespoon ketchup

   Soak mustard seeds in 1/4 cup of water for 1/2 hour. Blend to make a smooth paste. Beat the yogurt so that there will not be any lump left. Mix all the other ingredients except the chilies and 1/2 cup of water with the yogurt. Marinate the fish with the mixture. Leave it for 1/2 hour. Transfer everything to a microwave-safe pan. Place the chilies on top. Cook for 10 minutes on medium power with the lid on. Let it rest, and enjoy it with hot rice

Shrimp and Potato Curry (Serves Four)

1 pound medium or large shrimp, deveined and washed
2 medium potatoes, peeled and diccd
1 medium onion, chopped
1 medium tomato, chopped
1 tablespoon ginger paste or powder
1 tablespoon garlic paste or powder
1 1/2 teaspoon turmeric powder
1 teaspoon cumin powder
1 teaspoon coriander powder
1/2 teaspoon chili powder

1 teaspoon garam masala
6 tablespoons oil
1 1/2 teaspoon salt or to taste
1/2 teaspoon sugar
1 tablespoon ketchup

Marinate shrimp with 1/2 teaspoon of salt and 1/2 teaspoon of turmeric. Heat up oil in a pan and fry potatoes for 5 minutes. Set aside. Add the onion and fry until golden brown. Add ginger and garlic pastes and fry for a minute. Add the rest of the ingredients except ketchup and mix in medium heat for 5 minutes, stirring occasionally. Add potato pieces, shrimp, and ketchup. Mix everything for 5 minutes. Add 1 cup of water, and mix well. Cook in low heat for 10 minutes with the lid on. Let it stand. Serve.

Shrimp Malai Curry (Serves Four)

1 pound large shrimp, deveined and washed
1 medium onion, cubed
1 1-inch ginger, sliced
1 teaspoon cumin powder
1 teaspoon coriander powder
1 teaspoon turmeric
1/2 teaspoon chili powder
1 teaspoon garam masala
1/2 cup yogurt
1 cup coconut milk
6 tablespoons ghee or butter
1 1/2 teaspoon salt
1/2 teaspoon sugar
Dry spices: 1 bay leaf, 1 cinnamon stick, 2 cloves, 2 cardamom pods

Blend the onion and ginger and set aside. Beat yogurt and set aside. Marinate shrimp with 1/2 teaspoon of salt and 1/2 teaspoon of turmeric for 5 minutes. Heat up ghee in a pan and add all the dry spices and fry for a minute. Add the marinated shrimp and fry for 2 minutes and set aside. Add all the other ingredients except yogurt and coconut milk. Mix everything in medium heat until it looks dry and oil comes out. Add yogurt, and mix well for 2 minutes. Add shrimp and mix everything well. Pour the coconut milk and 1 cup of water, and mix well. Cook for 10 minutes in low heat with the lid on. Let it rest. Enjoy with hot rice.

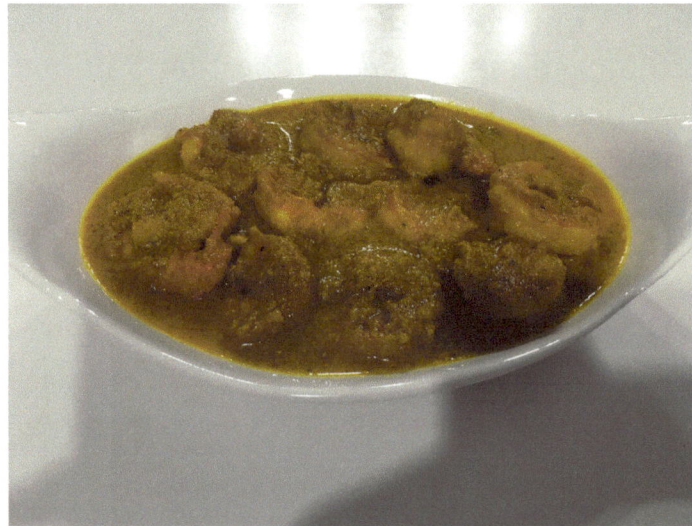

Steamed Shrimp with Coconut

1 pound medium shrimp, deveined and washed
1 cup grated fresh or dry coconut
1 tablespoon white mustard seeds
4 green chilies
4 tablespoons mustard or any other oil
1/2 teaspoon chili powder

1 teaspoon salt
1/2 teaspoon sugar

Soak the mustard seeds in 2 tablespoons of water for 1/2 hour. Blend it to a paste. Add coconut and 1/2 cup of water and blend well. Add all the other ingredients to the blend. Add shrimp, and mix well. Cook in the microwave for 10 minutes on medium power with the lid on. Mix well and let it rest and serve with hot rice.

Egg Curry (Serves Four)

4 eggs
1 medium onion, sliced
6 tablespoons oil
1 teaspoon salt or to taste
1 teaspoon turmeric powder
1/4 teaspoon chili powder
1 teaspoon ketchup

Boil eggs and peel them. Make small cuts on the eggs. Rub them with 1/4 teaspoon of salt and 1/4 teaspoon of turmeric. Heat up 2 tablespoons of oil and fry the eggs in medium heat for 2 minutes. Set aside. Heat up the rest of the oil and fry the sliced onion until golden brown. Add the rest of the ingredients, and mix well. Add the fried eggs. Mix everything well. Add 1/4 cup of water, and mix well. Cook for another 5 minutes in low heat with the lid on. Set aside. Serve.

Egg and Potato Curry (Serves Four)

4 eggs, boiled and peeled
2 medium potatoes, boiled and peeled
1 medium onion, sliced
1 medium tomato, chopped
1 tablespoon ginger paste or powder
1 tablespoon garlic paste or powder
1/2 teaspoon cumin powder
1/2 teaspoon coriander powder
1 teaspoon turmeric powder
1/2 teaspoon chili
1/2 teaspoon garam masala
6 tablespoons oil
1 1/2 teaspoon salt or to taste

Make small cuts on the eggs and cut the potatoes in half. Rub eggs with 1/4 teaspoon of salt and 1/4 teaspoon of turmeric. Heat up 2 tablespoons of oil and fry the eggs until golden brown. Set aside. Heat up the rest of the oil and fry the onion in medium heat until golden brown. Add ginger and garlic pastes and fry for a minute. Add all the other ingredients and mix everything in medium heat, stirring occasionally until it looks dry and oil comes out. Add potatoes and eggs. Mix well. Add 1/2 cup of water. Mix well. Cook in low heat for 5 minutes. Let it rest and serve.

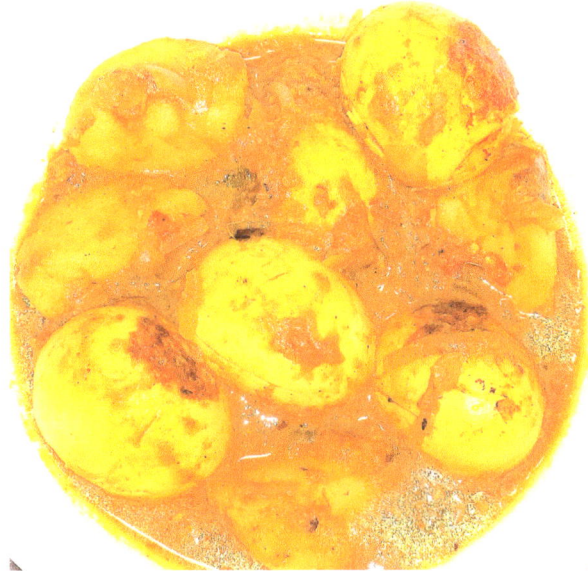

Spicy Omelet

2 eggs
4 tablespoons sliced onion
1 green chili, thinly sliced
2 tablespoons oil
Pinch of salt

Beat all ingredients together except oil. Heat up oil in a frying pan. Spread oil all over the pan. Pour the mixture into the pan and spread it all over. Cook for 2 minutes on each side in medium heat, pressing it with a spatula. Fold it and serve hot.

Spicy Scrambled Egg

2 eggs
4 tablespoons chopped onion
4 tablespoons chopped vegetables (any type)
1 green chili, thinly sliced
4 tablespoons oil
Pinch of salt

Beat the eggs, and set them aside. Heat up oil and fry onion slices for 2 minutes. Add vegetables and all the other ingredients and cook on medium heat for 2 minutes. Add eggs. Mix with vegetables. Cook for 5 minutes, stirring well until dry. Serve.

French Toast

4 slices bread (white or brown)
4 eggs
1/2 medium onion, thinly sliced
2 green chilies, thinly sliced
1/2 cup oil
1/2 teaspoon salt

Cut each slice of bread diagonally. Set aside. Beat eggs. Add salt, onion, and chilies to the eggs. Mix well. Heat up 2 tablespoons of oil in a frying pan. Take one slice of bread, and dip it in the egg mixture, and fry in medium heat until brown on both sides. While frying press the bread with your spatula so that the inside gets cooked well. Finish up frying the rest this way. Enjoy hot with ketchup or any of your favorite condiments.

SNACKS

Pappadam (Available in Indian Grocery Stores)

Microwaved Pappadam

Microwave the thinner pappadam for 30 seconds in high power and the thicker ones for 40 seconds.

Deep-Fried Pappadam

Spread paper towel on a tray. Heat up oil and hold each piece of raw pappadam with a tong and submerge in oil for a second. Do not fry for too long since it burns very fast. Place them on the tray to get rid of excess oil. Enjoy with dal and rice or as is.

Onion Pakora (Serves Four)

1 medium onion, thinly sliced
2 green chilies, chopped
1 tablespoon ginger paste or powder
1 cup gram flour (available in Indian grocery stores) or 3/4 cup bleached flour and 1/4 cup rice powder
1 teaspoon salt or to taste
1/2 teaspoon turmeric
1/2 cup thinly chopped cilantro
Oil for deep frying

Mix all ingredients except oil, adding 1/2 cup of water. Heat up oil in a pan, and take 1 tablespoon of mixture at a time, and fit in the pan as much as you can. Fry them in medium-high heat until brown on all sides. Finish up frying all of them this way. Serve hot with ketchup or any of your favorite condiments.

Onion can also be replaced with cabbage. In Calcutta, a very popular evening snack is rice crispy with pakoras accompanied by hot chai.

Aloo Chop (Potato Fritters)

2 medium potatoes, boiled
1 cup gram flour (available in Indian grocery stores) or 3/4 cup flour and 1/4 cup rice powder
1 tablespoon ginger paste or powder
1 tablespoon garlic paste or powder
1 teaspoon chili flakes
3/4 teaspoon turmeric powder

1 teaspoon salt or to taste
Oil for deep frying

Peel the boiled potatoes, and smash them very well. Heat up 2 tablespoons of oil in a pan. Add ginger and garlic pastes, 1/2 teaspoon of salt, and 1/2 teaspoon of turmeric and mix for 2 minutes in medium heat. Add the potatoes and mix everything very well. Set aside. Make batter using gram flour, 3/4 cup of water, and the rest of the salt and turmeric. Rub oil on both of your palms. Take 2 tablespoons of potato mix in your palms and make a ball. Flatten the ball to a 1/4-inch-thick circle. Take that out of your palms, and set it aside. Finish up making all the patties this way. Heat up oil for frying. Take one patty and dip it into the batter. Take the excess batter out and drop it in the oil. Fry in medium-high heat until brown on all sides. Finish up frying and serve hot.

In Calcutta rice crispy with aloo chop is a very popular evening snack taken with hot chai.

Cauliflower and Broccoli Fritters

1/2 cauliflower or broccoli, separated into 1-inch-size florets
1 cup gram flour (available in Indian grocery stores) or 3/4 cup bleached flour and 1/4 cup rice flour
3/4 teaspoon salt
3/4 teaspoon turmeric
1/2 teaspoon chili powder
3/4 cup water
Oil for deep frying

Marinate vegetables with 1/2 teaspoon of salt and 1/2 teaspoon of turmeric powder. Set aside for 10 minutes. Pat dry with a paper towel. Make batter using all the other ingredients except oil. Heat up oil. Dip the florets in the batter and fry in medium-high heat until brown on all sides. Serve hot.

Vegetable Chops

2 medium potatoes
2 medium fresh beets or 1 can beets
2 medium carrots
1/2 cup peas
1/4 cup roasted peanuts
1 tablespoon ginger paste or powder
1 teaspoon cumin powder
1 teaspoon coriander powder
1/2 teaspoon turmeric powder
1/2 teaspoon chili powder
1 teaspoon garam masala
1 1/2 teaspoon salt
1 teaspoon sugar
1 tablespoon ketchup
Oil for deep frying
2 eggs
1 cup flour
2 cups bread crumbs

Cut each beet into eight pieces. Pressure-cook the whole potatoes, whole carrots, and beet pieces for 15 minutes. Let them get cold and peel them. Smash the beet pieces thoroughly and squeeze the water out. Set aside. Smash potatoes and carrots in a microwave-safe pot. Add beets and all the other ingredients except peanuts, eggs, flour, and bread crumbs. Add 2 tablespoons of oil and mix everything well. Cook in the microwave uncovered for 10 minutes. Take it out and mix very well. Cook for some more time until the mixture feels dry. Let it cool completely. Beat the eggs, and set them aside. Rub oil on both of your palms. Separate the dough into golf ball-size pieces. Take one piece in your palms and give it the shape of a ball and then flatten it a little. You can also give it an oval shape. Finish up making the chops, and set them aside. Take one chop at a time and cover it with flour. Shake off the excess flour, dip it in the egg, and cover it with bread crumbs. Repeat this process for all of them. Heat up oil to medium-high. Deep-fry them in medium-high heat until brown on all sides. Serve hot with any condiments of your choice and cucumber and onion slices.

Fish Fry

1 pound tilapia fillet (fresh or frozen)
1/4 medium onion
1 1-inch-size fresh ginger
2 big cloves garlic
1 teaspoon garam masala
2 green chilies
1/2 cup chopped cilantro
4 tablespoons lime juice
1 1/2 teaspoon salt
2 eggs
1 cup flour
2 cups bread crumbs
Oil for deep frying

Cut the fillet into 3-inch-size pieces. Set aside. Make a paste of onion, ginger, garlic, cilantro, and chilies. Add all the other ingredients to the paste except eggs, flour, and bread crumbs. Marinate the fish with this mixture. Keep in the fridge overnight. The next day, take the fish out 2 hours before cooking. Beat the eggs. Take one piece of fish, and cover it with flour. Shake off the excess flour and dip in eggs. Cover it with bread crumbs. Prepare all the pieces this way. Heat up oil and fry them in medium-high heat until brown on both sides. Serve hot.

Tuna Chop

10 ounces canned tuna
2 medium potatoes, boiled
1 medium onion, chopped
1 tablespoon ginger paste or powder

1 tablespoon garlic paste or powder
1/2 teaspoon turmeric powder
1 teaspoon chili powder
1 teaspoon garam masala
1 teaspoon salt
1/4 teaspoon sugar
1/2 cup thinly chopped cilantro
Oil for deep frying
2 eggs beaten
1 cup flour
1 cup bread crumbs

Peel potatoes and smash them. Open the can of tuna and squeeze out the oil or water. Set aside. Heat up 4 tablespoons of oil in a pan. Fry the onion until golden brown. Add all the ingredients except cilantro, eggs, flour, and bread crumbs. Mix everything for 5 minutes in medium heat. Add the tuna, and mix well for 5 minutes. Add potatoes and cilantro and mix everything well. Let it cool. Rub oil on both palms. Take 3 tablespoons of mixture in your palms. Roll it to a ball and flatten it a little. Finish up making all the circles this way. Beat the eggs well. Take one round and cover it with flour. Shake off the excess flour. Dip it in the eggs. Cover it with bread crumbs. Finish up preparing all of them. Heat up oil in a frying pan. Fry them in medium-high heat until brown on both sides. Serve hot with ketchup.

Chicken Cutlets

1 pound chicken breasts
1/4 medium onion
1 1-inch-size ginger
2 big cloves garlic
2 fresh green chilies
1 teaspoon garam masala

1/2 cup chopped cilantro
4 tablespoons lime juice
1 1/2 teaspoon salt
2 eggs
1 cup flour
2 cups bread crumbs
Oil for deep frying

Cut breasts into 4-inch-size thin pieces. Make a paste of onion, ginger, garlic, chilies, and cilantro. Mix all the other ingredients with the paste except eggs, flour, and bread crumbs. Marinate the chicken pieces with this mixture, and keep them in the fridge overnight. The next day take it out 2 hours before cooking. Beat eggs and set aside. Take one chicken piece and cover it with flour. Shake the excess flour off and dip it in the eggs. Take it out of the eggs, and cover it with bread crumbs. Prepare all the pieces this way. Set aside. Heat up oil and deep-fry in medium-high heat until brown on both sides. Serve hot with ketchup and onion slices.

Kabab

1 pound ground turkey or chicken
1 medium onion, minced
1 1/2 tablespoons ginger paste or powder
1 1/2 tablespoons garlic paste or powder
1/2 teaspoon turmeric
1 tablespoon garam masala

1 1/2 teaspoon salt
1 teaspoon chili powder
1/2 cup regular bread crumbs
1 cup thinly chopped cilantro
2 tablespoons lime juice
1/2 cup oil

Mix all ingredients with the meat except oil. Set aside for an hour to marinate. Rub oil on your palms. Take 3 tablespoons of the mix in your palms and make a ball and flatten it a little. Finish up making all the patties this way. Set them aside. Heat up half of the oil in a frying pan and spread it all over the pan. Place as many patties as you can fit in the pan. Fry in medium heat until brown on each side. Take them out. Add the rest of the oil and repeat the process. Serve hot.

Chicken Tikka (Serves Four)

2 pounds chicken breasts
1 medium onion
1 bell pepper
3/4 cup yogurt
2 tablespoons lime juice
1 tablespoon ginger paste or powder
1 tablespoon garlic paste or powder

1 teaspoon chili powder
1 1/2 teaspoons salt
4 tablespoons oil

Cut chicken breasts into 1-inch-size cubes. Cut the onion and bell paper into 1-inch-size pieces. Mix all the ingredients together. Marinate chicken and vegetable pieces with the spice mix. Let it rest for 3 hours. You can use either metal or wooden skewers. If you are using wooden ones, soak them in water for an hour before using them. Skew one chicken piece first and then one or two onion pieces followed by one or two bell pepper pieces. Assemble chicken and vegetable pieces this way. Heat up the oven to 350 degrees. Wrap a baking tray with foil. Keep the skewers on the baking tray. Bake each side for 20 minutes, occasionally basting the chicken and vegetable pieces with the rest of the marinade. Serve hot with lemon wedges.

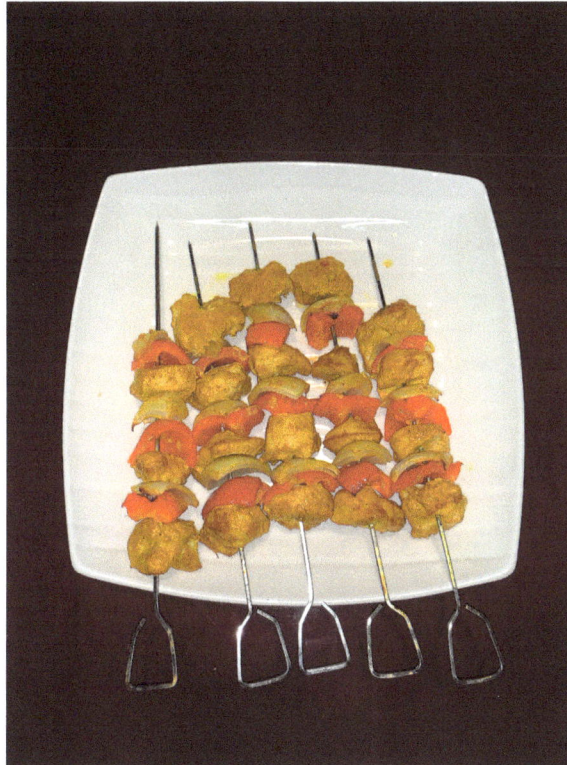

Spicy Rice Crispy

4 cups rice crispy
1 cup Indian trail mix (available in Indian stores)
1/2 cup minced onion
1 green chili, thinly sliced
1/2 cup thinly chopped cilantro
1 medium potato, boiled and diced small
1/2 cup garbanzo beans, boiled

1/4 teaspoon salt

2 teaspoons mustard oil (optional)

Mix the potato and garbanzo beans with salt. Set aside. Mix all the other ingredients very well. Add the potato and garbanzo beans. Mix well. Serve with tea.

This is one of the most popular evening snacks in Calcutta.

Spicy Pancakes

1 cup pancake mix
3/4 cup milk
1 egg
6 tablespoons oil
1/2 medium onion, minced
1 green chili, chopped, or 1 teaspoon chili flakes
1/2 teaspoon salt

    Mix everything and 2 tablespoons of oil to make the batter. Heat up the frying pan and spread 1 teaspoon of oil over the pan. Pour 4 tablespoons of batter and cook for 2 minutes on each side on medium-high heat. Finish up making all the pancakes this way. Enjoy with Indian pickle or any of your favorite condiments.

BREAD

Roti (Makes Four)

1 cup unbleached flour
1/2 cup water

Make a dough starting with 1/4 cup of water and gradually adding the rest. Knead the dough for at least 10 minutes until soft and not sticky. Add more flour if the dough turns watery. Divide the dough into four portions. Take one portion in your palms and make a ball. Sprinkle 1 tablespoon of flour on the rolling board and press the ball on the board and flatten it. Roll each ball into an 8-inch-size circle. Shake off the excess flour. Heat up a frying pan, which is thick at the bottom. Put the raw roti on the frying pan at high temperature. Roast for 1 minute. Turn sides and roast for another minute. Take 2 paper towels and fold them together. Hold the paper towels with your fingers and slowly press all different parts of the roti until it becomes fluffy on both sides but not burnt. Rub with butter and enjoy hot with any curry.

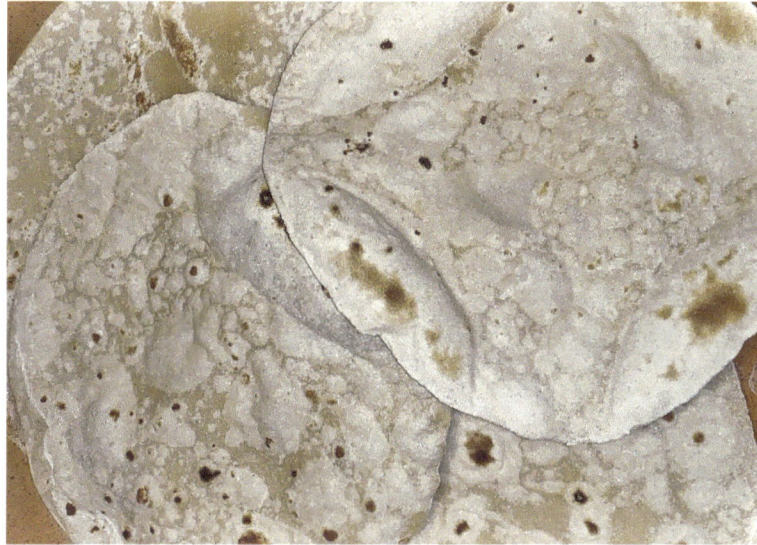

Naan (Indian Bread)

3 cups flour
2 teaspoon baking powder
1/2 teaspoon baking soda
1 teaspoon salt
1 teaspoon sugar
2 tablespoons oil
1 cup warm milk
1/2 cup water

Mix all the dry ingredients together. Pour milk, and mix well. Make a dough adding 2 tablespoons of water at a time. Knead the dough for at least 10 minutes. The dough should be soft and not sticky. Add more flour if needed. Brush the dough with oil and wrap it in plastic. Set aside for 1/2 hour. Divide the dough into six portions. Take one portion of the dough and make a ball, rolling it in your palms. Add 1 tablespoon of flour to the rolling board and press the ball on the board and flatten it. Roll it into a circle or oval, 1/4 inch thick and 8 inches in diameter. Finish up rolling all the balls this way. Keep the oven rack 8 inches away from the broiler. Turn the broiler to high and place the naans on the rack. Cook each side for 4 minutes. Rub butter on one side and wrap them in foil to keep warm.

Plain Paratha

2 cups unbleached flour
1/2 cup oil
1/4 teaspoon salt
1 cup water

Mix flour, 2 tablespoons of oil, and salt. Make a dough, gradually adding water. Knead the dough for 10 minutes until soft and not sticky. Divide the dough into six portions. Take one portion of the dough and make a ball, rolling it in your palms. Add 1 tablespoon of flour to the rolling board. Press the ball on the board and flatten it. Roll the ball into a thin circle, 8 inches in diameter. Heat up the frying pan to medium-high. Add the raw paratha to the pan and toast both sides for 1 minute each. Add 2 tablespoons of oil to the pan and fry the paratha for 2 minutes, pressing on it with a spatula. Turn it around and spread 2 tablespoons of oil on it. Fry the rest the same way and enjoy hot.

Egg Paratha

2 cups bleached flour
3 eggs
1/2 medium onion, thinly sliced
1/4-inch ginger, grated
1 green chili, thinly sliced
1 cup oil

3/4 teaspoon salt
3/4 cup water

Mix 1 egg, 1/2 teaspoon of salt, and 2 tablespoons of oil with the flour. Make a dough, gradually adding water. Knead the dough for at least 10 minutes. The dough should be soft but not sticky. Add more flour if needed. Set aside. Mix 2 eggs, onion, ginger, chili, and the rest of the salt. Set aside. Divide the dough into four pieces. Take one piece and make a ball, rolling it in your palms. Add 1 tablespoon of flour to the rolling board and press one ball on the rolling board. Flatten it with your fingers. Now roll it to a very thin circle, approximately 12–14 inches in diameter. Pour 1/4 of the egg mix in the middle. Spread it. Fold all four sides, covering the egg mix, and form a square. Heat up 4 tablespoons of oil in a frying pan. Transfer the paratha to the pan by holding four corners together so that you do not spill the liquid. Fry each side for 2–3 minutes by pressing the paratha with your spatula. Take it out. Add more oil and repeat. Finish up cooking all four parathas and serve hot with ketchup and cucumber and onion slices.

Puffed Bread (Luchi)

2 cups flour
1/4 teaspoon salt
Oil for deep frying
3/4 cup water

Mix flour, salt, and 2 tablespoons of oil. Make a dough, gradually adding water. Knead the dough very well until soft and not sticky. Add more flour if needed. Divide the dough into sixteen portions. Make balls by rolling them in your palms. Take one ball and press it on your rolling board. Add 2–3 drops of oil to the flattened ball, and roll it into a 4-inch-size circle. Finish up making the circles. Heat up oil in a deep pan or wok. Fry the luchis on each side for a minute in high heat. Finish up frying all the luchis this way. Enjoy hot with any curry.

Potato Paratha

2 cups whole wheat
2 medium potatoes
1/2 medium onion, minced
1 tablespoon ginger paste or powder
1 tablespoon garlic paste or powder
1 teaspoon chili
1 teaspoon salt
1/2 teaspoon sugar
2 tablespoons thinly chopped cilantro
1 cup oil
1 cup water

Mix the whole wheat with 1/2 teaspoon of salt, 1/2 teaspoon of sugar, and 2 tablespoons of oil. Make a dough, gradually adding water. Knead the dough for at least 10 minutes. The dough should be soft and not sticky. Add more flour if needed. Keep it covered for at least 1/2 hour. Boil potatoes. Peel and smash them. Heat up 2 tablespoons of oil in a pan. Fry the minced onion on medium heat until golden brown. Add ginger and garlic pastes and mix for a minute. Add all the other ingredients and cook for 2 minutes. Add the potatoes, and mix well. Let it cool. Make eight balls out of the potato mix, rolling them in your palms. Make eight balls out of the dough the same way. Take one flour ball and flatten it on your palm. Take one potato ball and place it in the middle of the flour ball. Completely cover the potato ball with the flour ball and seal it. Make a smooth ball by rolling it in your palms. Add 1 tablespoon of flour to the rolling board. Press the ball on the board and roll it to a thin circle, 8 inches in diameter. Finish up rolling all the balls this way. Heat up a thick frying pan in medium-high heat and place a raw paratha and cook for a minute on each side. Add 2 tablespoons of oil or ghee to the pan. Fry parathas for 2 minutes each side in medium heat, pressing it with a spatula. Turn the side. Add 2 tablespoons of oil and fry the same way. Finish up frying all of them. Enjoy hot.

RICE

White Basmati Rice on Stove Top

Soak 1 cup of rice in water for half an hour. Wash and rinse thoroughly. Add 6 cups of warm water and let it boil in high heat with the lid on. When the water starts boiling, take the lid off and turn the temperature to medium-high and boil for 10 to 15 minutes. Take one grain in a spoon and check if it is done or not. If not, boil for some more time. Pour everything in a colander under running water in the sink.

Drain the water out for 5 minutes. Serve hot.

Brown Basmati Rice on Stove Top

Soak 1 cup of rice in water for an hour. Wash and rinse thoroughly. Add 6 cups of warm water and let it boil in high heat with the lid on. Once the water starts boiling, take the lid off and turn the heat to medium-high and boil for 20 minutes. Pour the rice into a colander under running water in the sink, and drain the water for 5 minutes. Enjoy hot.

This procedure helps take out the extra starch from the rice, making it low in calories.

White Basmati Rice in Microwave

Soak 1 cup of rice in water for half an hour. Wash and rinse thoroughly. Add 2 cups of water, and mix well. Cook in the microwave for 15 minutes on medium power, uncovered. Take it out. Cover it and let it stand for 5 minutes and serve.

Brown Rice in Microwave

Soak 1 cup of rice for an hour. Wash and rinse thoroughly. Add 3 cups of water, and cook for 20 minutes on medium power.

Rice with Peas

1 cup rice
1 cup peas
1/4 teaspoon cumin seeds
1/2 teaspoon salt
2 tablespoons oil or ghee

Soak rice for half an hour. Wash and drain the water. Heat up oil in a pan and fry the cumin seeds for 2 seconds. Add peas and fry for 2 minutes, adding salt. Add the washed rice and mix everything well. Add 2 cups of water. Mix well. Start cooking in high heat with the lid on. When the water starts boiling, turn the heat to low and boil the rice for 10 minutes with the lid on. Open the lid and mix everything very lightly with a fork. Serve hot.

Sweet Yellow Rice

1 cup basmati rice
1/4 cup cashews, roasted
1/4 cup raisins
Dry spices: 1 bay leaf, 1-inch cinnamon stick, 2 cloves, 2 cardamom pods
1/2 teaspoon salt or to taste
1 1/2 tablespoons sugar
4 tablespoons oil or ghee
Yellow food color

Soak rice for 1/2 hour. Wash and rinse well. Heat up oil or ghee in a pan. Add all the dry spices and cashews and fry them until brown. Pour the rice into the pan. Add raisins. Mix everything well for another 2 minutes. Add all the other ingredients, 4 drops of food color, and 2 cups of water, and mix well. Cook in high heat with the lid on. Once the water starts boiling, turn the heat down to low and cook for 10 minutes covered. Mix very lightly and serve with any vegetarian or nonvegetarian dishes.

Vegetable Fried Rice

1 cup basmati rice
1/2 medium onion, thinly sliced
2 carrots, diced very small
1/2 cup peas
1/4 cup raisins
1 green chili, thinly sliced
1 teaspoon ginger paste
2 tablespoons butter or ghee
1 bay leaf, 1-inch-size cinnamon stick
2 cloves, 2 cardamom pods
1/2 teaspoon salt or to taste
1/2 teaspoon sugar

Soak the rice for 1/2 hour. Wash and rinse well. Set aside. Heat up butter in a pan. Fry all the dry spices for 2 minutes. Add vegetables, raisins, salt, and sugar and fry for 5 minutes in medium heat. Add chili and ginger and rice. Mix well. Add 2 cups of water and start cooking in high heat. Once the water starts boiling, turn the heat to low and cook for 10 minutes covered. Let it rest and mix lightly with a fork. Serve hot.

Khichuri (Vegetarian Jambalaya)

1 cup basmati rice
1/2 cup red or masoor dal
1/2 cup mung or yellow dal
1 medium onion, sliced
2 tablespoons ginger paste or powder
1 teaspoon cumin powder
1 teaspoon coriander powder
1 teaspoon turmeric
1/2 teaspoon chili powder
1 teaspoon garam masala
2 green chilies, slit in the middle
2 cups frozen mixed vegetables
1 1/2 teaspoons salt or to taste
1/2 teaspoon sugar
4 tablespoons oil
1 tablespoon ghee

Wash and rinse rice and dal. Set aside. Heat up oil in a big pan and fry the onion until golden brown. Add all the ingredients except garam masala, ghee, and vegetables and mix them until it is dry and oil comes out. Add the washed rice and dal, and mix well. Add 8 cups of water, and mix well. Cook for 20 minutes in medium heat with the lid on. Add vegetables and cook for 5 more minutes. If it ends up with too much liquid, cook for 10 more minutes without the lid. Add ghee and garam masala, and mix well. Set aside and serve with pakora, fried eggplant, and omelet.

Recipes of all these accompaniments are here in the book.

Chicken Biryani

2 pounds chicken with bones
3 medium onions, thinly sliced
1 1/2 tablespoons ginger paste
1 1/2 tablespoons garlic paste
1 teaspoon cumin powder
1 teaspoon coriander powder
1 teaspoon turmeric
1 teaspoon chili powder
1 teaspoon garam masala
1/2 cup yogurt
1 tablespoon salt
1/2 cup oil
4 tablespoons butter or ghee

2 cups basmati rice
1/2 cup milk
4 drops yellow food color
Dry spices: 2 bay leaves, 1 cinnamon stick, 2 cloves, 2 cardamom pods
1 cup finely chopped cilantro

Cut chicken into 2-inch-size pieces. Marinate them with 1 tablespoon of ginger paste, 1 tablespoon of garlic paste, 1/2 tablespoon of salt, turmeric, and yogurt. Set aside for an hour. Mix food color with the milk and set aside. Soak rice in water for half an hour. Heat up oil. Add onion slices and fry them very well. Take out 1/2 of the fried onions for later use. Add the marinated chicken and all the other spices except ghee, milk, dry spices, and cilantro. Cook in medium heat, stirring occasionally until the mixture looks dry and oil comes out. Add 1/2 cup of water. Mix well. Cook for 10 minutes in low heat with the lid on. Wash and rinse rice. Add 8 cups of water, 2 tablespoons of salt, and all the dry spices. Cook rice for 6–8 minutes in medium-high heat until rice is 80 percent done. Drain water. Melt the butter or ghee. Rub a pan with 1 tablespoon of butter or ghee. Take half of the chicken along with gravy and spread at the bottom of the pan. Spread half of the rice on top of the chicken. Add half of the fried onion, half of the colored milk, and half of the chopped cilantro. Repeat the same process of arranging rice and chicken. Add the rest of the melted ghee over the top layer. Cover the pan and cook for 10 minutes on low heat. Gently remove the biryani from the pan and enjoy with yogurt relish or raita.

Goat Biryani

2 pounds goat with bones
4 medium onions, thinly sliced
2 tablespoons ginger paste
2 tablespoons garlic paste
1 teaspoon cumin powder

1 teaspoon coriander powder
1 teaspoon chili powder
1 teaspoon garam masala
1 teaspoon turmeric powder
4 green chilies, cut in the middle
1/2 cup oil
1/2 cup yogurt
1 tablespoon salt
2 cups basmati rice
4 tablespoons ghee or butter
Dry spices: 1 bay leaf, 1 cinnamon stick, 2 cloves, 4 cardamom pods
1/2 cup chopped cilantro
1/2 cup milk
4 drops yellow food color

Cut the meat into 2-inch-size pieces. Marinate them with 1 tablespoon of ginger, 1 tablespoon of garlic, turmeric, garam masala, yogurt, and 1/2 tablespoon of salt. Set aside for 4 hours. Mix food color with the milk. Set aside. Soak rice for 1/2 hour and set aside. Heat up oil in a pan and fry the sliced onions until golden brown. Take out 1/2 of the onions for later use. Add the marinated meat and the rest of the ingredients except ghee, milk, dry spices, and cilantro. Cook everything for 15 minutes in medium heat, stirring occasionally until oil comes out. Add little water if the mixture starts getting stuck at the bottom. Add 1 1/2 cups of water. Mix well. Pressure-cook for 20 minutes. If the meat is left with a lot of water, cook for 5 more minutes in medium heat uncovered. Wash and rinse the rice. Add 10 cups of water, 2 tablespoons of salt, and all the dry whole spices. Mix well. Cook rice for 8 minutes on medium heat. Drain the rice. Set aside. Melt ghee or butter. Brush the bottom of a nonstick pan with 1 tablespoon of ghee. Add half of the goat curry to the bottom of the pan. Spread it evenly. Evenly spread half of the rice on top of the meat. Sprinkle 1/2 of the fried onions and evenly pour 1/2 cup of colored milk and 1 tablespoon of ghee. Spread the rest of the meat and the rice the same way as before. Cook for 10 minutes in low heat with the lid on. Let it rest. Lightly mix the meat and the rice. Serve with raita or yogurt relish.

SALAD

Beet Salad

1 medium beet, peeled and grated
1 carrot, peeled and grated
1 medium-size cucumber, peeled and chopped
1/2 medium onion, chopped
1 green chili, thinly sliced
1 tablespoon lime juice
1/2 teaspoon salt or to taste
4 tablespoons chopped cilantro

Mix everything well and serve.

Carrot and Cucumber Salad

1 big carrot, peeled and thinly sliced
1 cucumber, thinly sliced
1/2 medium onion, thinly sliced
1/2 cup vinegar
1 teaspoon chili flakes

3/4 teaspoon salt or to taste
1 teaspoon sugar

Mix all ingredients well except the vegetables. Pour the mixture on the vegetables, and mix well. Let it rest for an hour and serve.

Cucumber and Tomato Salad

1 medium cucumber, peeled and diced small
2 medium tomatoes, diced small
1/2 medium onion, diced small
1 green chili, thinly sliced
1 tablespoon lime juice
1/2 teaspoon salt or to taste
1/4 teaspoon sugar
4 tablespoons chopped cilantro

Mix everything well. Serve.

Carrot Salad

4 medium carrots, grated
2 green chilies, thinly sliced
6 tablespoons vinegar
3/4 teaspoon salt or to taste
1/2 teaspoon sugar

Mix everything well. Let it rest for an hour and serve.

Apple Chutney

4 apples
Pinch of salt
Pinch of turmeric
3/4 cup sugar
1 teaspoon oil
1/2 teaspoon roasted cumin powder
1 dry chili or 1/4 teaspoon chili powder
1 teaspoon lime juice

Slice each apple into six wedges. Heat up oil in a pan and fry the chili for a minute. Add apple pieces and fry for 2 minutes, adding salt and turmeric. Cook apples in low heat with the lid on until soft. Sprinkle little water if needed. Add sugar, and mix well. Cook for another 10 minutes in low heat without the lid. Let it rest for 5 minutes. Add lime juice and roasted cumin powder. Mix well. Set aside and enjoy.

Apple can be replaced with peach and apricot.

Tomato Chutney

4 medium tomatoes, chopped
1/2 cup raisins
1/4 teaspoon salt
1/4 teaspoon turmeric
1 cup sugar
1 teaspoon oil
1/2 teaspoon roasted cumin powder
1/4 teaspoon chili powder

Heat up oil in a pan. Add tomatoes, salt, and turmeric and mix for a minute. Cook for 5 minutes in medium heat with the lid on. Add sugar, raisins, and chili powder, and mix well. Cook for 10 more minutes in low heat uncovered, stirring occasionally. Add roasted cumin powder. Mix well. Let it rest and serve.

Mango Chutney

2 raw mangoes, sliced in 1/2-inch-thick wedges
1/2 teaspoon salt
1/4 teaspoon turmeric
1 1/2 cups sugar
1/4 teaspoon chili powder
1/2 teaspoon roasted cumin powder
1 teaspoon oil
1 teaspoon lime juice

Marinate the mango pieces with salt and turmeric. Set aside for 1/2 hour. Heat up oil and fry the mango pieces for a minute. Add 1/4 cup of water, and mix well. Cook in low heat for 5 minutes with the lid on. Add sugar, and mix well. Cook for another 10 minutes in low heat without the lid. Add cumin and chili powder. Mix well. Let it cool. Add lime juice. Serve.

Pineapple Chutney

1/2 pineapple, peeled and grated
1 cup sugar
1 pinch salt
1 tablespoon lime juice
1 teaspoon oil
1/4 cup raisins

Heat up oil in a pan and add pineapple and salt. Mix well. Cook for 5 minutes in low heat with the lid on. Take the lid off and add sugar. Cook for 10 more minutes in low heat without the lid. Mix the lime juice and let it cool. Enjoy.

Raw Papaya Chutney

1 medium raw papaya
1 1/2 cups sugar
A pinch of salt
2 tablespoons lime juice
1 teaspoon oil

Peel the papaya and take out the seeds from inside. Cut it into six pieces vertically. Slice each piece horizontally very thin. Heat up oil in a frying pan and add papaya slices and salt and mix for a minute. Cook in low heat with the lid on until papaya slices are half-cooked. Sprinkle little water if needed, making sure that it is not getting burnt at the bottom. Add sugar and cook for 15 minutes in medium heat without the lid. At this point, the papaya pieces should look translucent. If not, cook a little longer the same way. Add lime juice, and mix well. Let it rest. Enjoy.

In the end, the papaya pieces look like plastic. That is why this chutney is known as plastic chutney in Calcutta.

Coriander Chutney

1 bunch fresh coriander
2 fresh green chilies
4 tablespoons lime juice
1/2 teaspoon salt or to taste
2 teaspoons sugar

Wash coriander leaves thoroughly. Blend the leaves and chilies together, adding 4 tablespoons of water. Add all the other ingredients, and mix well. Enjoy.

Yogurt Relish (Raita)

2 cups yogurt
1/4 teaspoon salt or to taste
2 tablespoons sugar
1 cucumber, grated
1 carrot, grated
1/2 teaspoon roasted cumin
1/2 teaspoon chili powder

Squeeze water out of the grated cucumber and carrot. Set aside. Beat the yogurt, adding 1/4 cup of water. Add all the other ingredients, and mix well. Add the grated cucumber and carrot to the yogurt. Mix well and enjoy.

Yogurt with Garbanzo Beans

2 cups yogurt
3/4 cup boiled beans
1/4 teaspoon salt or to taste
2 tablespoons sugar or to taste
1/2 teaspoon roasted cumin powder
1/2 teaspoon chili powder

Beat yogurt, adding 1/4 cup of water. Add all ingredients, and mix well. Enjoy.

Yogurt with Potatoes

2 cups yogurt
2 medium boiled potatoes, peeled and cubed small
1/2 teaspoon salt or to taste
2 tablespoons sugar or to taste
1/2 teaspoon roasted cumin powder
1/2 teaspoon chili powder

Beat the yogurt, adding 1/2 cup of water. Add all ingredients except potatoes. Mix well. Add potatoes, and mix well. Serve.

DESSERTS

Gulab Jamun

2 cups milk powder
2 tablespoons flour
1/4 teaspoon baking powder
3/4 cup half-and-half
2 cups sugar
2 1/2 cups water
Oil to deep fry

Boil sugar and water for 10 minutes to make the sugar syrup. Set it aside. Mix the dry ingredients well. Make a dough, gradually adding the milk. The dough needs to be very tight; otherwise, it will break while frying. Break the dough into twelve portions. Make small tight balls, rolling them in your palms, and set them aside. Heat up oil in a deep pan or wok so that the balls can get submerged in oil completely while frying. Turn the heat to low before frying. Otherwise, the milk balls will get burnt outside, and the inside will not get cooked. Add six balls at a time and fry turning sides until they look dark brown on all sides and become double in size. Take them out of the oil, and soak them in the syrup for 12 hours. Enjoy.

Rice Pudding (Payesh)

3 cups half-and-half milk
1/2 cup basmati rice
1 1/2 cups sugar (white or brown)
1 tablespoon ghee or butter
A pinch of salt
2 bay leaves

1/2 cup raisins
2 cardamom pods

Soak the rice for 1/2 hour. Wash and dry the rice. Set aside. Heat up the milk in a heavy bottom pan. Rub the rice with ghee. Add the rice, and mix well. Cook in low heat, stirring occasionally until the rice is soft. Add all the other ingredients and give it a stir. Keep cooking until the milk is reduced to 1 cup. Let it cool and serve.

Halwa (Suji or Cream of Wheat)

1 cup cream of wheat
1 1/2 cups sugar
1 pinch salt
1 cup milk

1 cup water
6 tablespoons ghee or butter
3/4 cup cashews
1/2 cup raisins

Heat up 2 tablespoons of butter or ghee in low heat. Lightly fry the cashews, and set them aside. Heat up the rest of the ghee and add the cream of wheat and fry in medium heat until lightly brown. Add milk and water, and mix well. Add sugar and cook for 10 minutes in medium heat stirring frequently. Add cashews and raisins, and mix well. Enjoy.

Sweet Yogurt

32 ounces plain yogurt
1 can evaporated milk
1 can condensed milk

Mix these ingredients together in an oven-safe container. Heat up the oven to 500 degrees and turn it off. Place the container in the oven uncovered for 12 hours. Put it in the fridge to cool off and serve.

My utmost hope is that all my readers will find my book interesting and they will try these recipes whenever time permits. I believe following these recipes will enable them to make their friends and families very happy.

ABOUT THE AUTHOR

Anita Mallick grew up in an extended family, which included her grandmother, dad, mom, three aunts, one uncle, and twin brothers. She thinks that growing up with so many people under the same roof was the best thing that has happened to her. She was always under the radar of six to seven adults. As a result, breaking rules was never an option. Anita used to spend most of her day with her grandmother. Her grandmother was a great cook. Anita grew up watching everything her grandma did all day long. This cookbook is an inspiration from her, to say the least.

Anita earned her master's degree in philosophy from the University of Calcutta in 1981. She got married to a mechanical engineer in 1984. At that time, her husband was working in Baghdad, Iraq, and she joined him there. As she had not been away from Calcutta her entire life, it was quite a leap. In 1985 her husband resigned and planned to come to the United States for higher studies. Fayetteville, Arkansas, was their first stop since her husband was to join the MBA program at the University of Arkansas. One of the most crowded cities on earth, Fayetteville looked like a ghost town to her.

So far, Anita has lived in five different states due to her husband's job. Every day was a learning challenge to fit into a foreign system. Around this time her son and daughter were born. She was a stay-at-home mom at that time. And she used to keep herself busy with supervising her children, entertaining their friends, and doing things she always enjoyed doing, such as cooking and entertaining guests, doing arts and crafts, and volunteering in schools and churches.

Currently, she lives in Edina, Minnesota, with her husband. Her husband teaches MBA classes at the University of St. Thomas. Her kids attended Edina middle and high schools. They earned their engineering degrees from Johns Hopkins University. Her son is working in Baltimore, and her daughter is in Arizona. Her granddaughter, Ariane, was born on December 25, 2021. She is a bundle of joy in their life. Now Anita is working as an assistant teacher in a public school setting. She cherishes being with the kids. She also teaches cooking classes for adults and the youth in the Edina school system.

CPSIA information can be obtained
at www.ICGtesting.com
Printed in the USA
BVHW060535060223
657796BV00003B/7